*For Matthew, Charlie, Jack and Sally*

First published 1993 by
Walker Books Ltd
87 Vauxhall Walk
London SE11 5HJ

© 1993 Catherine and Laurence Anholt

This book has been typeset in Bembo.

Printed and bound in Italy by LEGO, Vicenza

British Library Cataloguing in Publication Data
A catalogue record for this book is
available from the British Library.
ISBN 0-7445-2546-2

# Here come the
# BABIES

*Catherine and Laurence Anholt*

WALKER BOOKS
LONDON

# Here come the babies!

Babies in boxes, babies in boots, babies on backs

Babies in socks, babies in suits, babies in sacks

# Babies everywhere!

Babies in coats, babies in cribs, babies with cats

Babies in boats, babies in bibs, babies with bats

# What are babies like?

Babies kick and babies crawl,

Slide their potties down the hall.

Babies smile and babies yell,

This one has a funny smell.

# What do babies look like?

Wriggles and dribbles and sticking out ears,

Little round faces with rivers of tears.

Babies wear suits which are long at the toes,

They stick out in the middle and up at the nose.

# What are mornings like?

Mum and Dad are fast asleep
And all the house is quiet.
I slip into baby's room
And start a little riot.

# What are mealtimes like?

Baby throwing tantrums,
Baby throwing fits,
Baby throwing dinner
In little baby bits.

# What do babies play with?

Bobbles and bows,

fingers and toes,

Shoes and hats,

sleeping cats,

Frizzy hair,

saggy bear,

Empty box,

Daddy's socks.

# What do babies dream of?

Pat-a-cake, pat-a-cake, dickory dock,
Wee Willie Winkie, it's past eight o'clock.

Hey diddle diddle and Little Bo-peep,
Bye Baby Bunting is counting sheep.

# What's in a pram?

nappy bag

favourite rag

food to cook

picture book

floppy bunny

something funny

one shoe

baby too

# What are two babies like?

Twins, twins,
Alike as two pins,
Double the trouble…

But double the grins!

# What is bathtime like?

Babies in a bubble bath,
Building with the bubbles,

Bubbly beards and bubbly hair
And great big bubbly puddles.

# What does a baby do?

hug

hold

hide

sleep

smile

slide

| | | |
|---|---|---|
| jumble | juggle | jump |
| bang | burp | bump |
| totter | tumble | throw |
| gurgle | giggle | grow |

# What do lots of babies do?

One baby bouncing on her brother's knee,

Two in a play-pen, three by the sea,

Four babies yelling while their
mummies try to talk,

Five babies, holding hands,
learning how to walk.

# What do *we* do?

Tickle tummies, dry up tears,

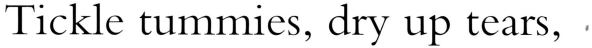

Whisper secrets in their ears, then...

Bed for baby
And me too,
Bye-bye, baby. I love
You.